FOCUS ON THE FAMILY ®

HELP!
SOMEONE I LOVE IS DEPRESSED

HELP!
SOMEONE I LOVE IS DEPRESSED

dr. bill maier
general editor

archibald d. hart, ph.d.
author

Tyndale House Publishers, Inc.
Carol Stream, Illinois

A Focus on the Family book published by
Tyndale House Publishers, Carol Stream, Illinois 60188

TYNDALE and Tyndale's quill logo are registered trademarks of Tyndale House
Publishers, Inc.

People's names and certain details of cases mentioned in this book have
been changed to protect the privacy of the individuals involved. However, the author has attempted to convey the essence of the experience
and the underlying principles as accurately as possible.

Editors: Larry Weeden and Kathy Davis
Cover design by: Joseph Sapulich
Cover photograph © by Rosanne Olson/Getty Images. All rights reserved.

Library of Congress Cataloging-in-Publication Data
Hart, Archibald D.
  Help! Someone I love is depressed / Archibald D. Hart ; Bill Maier,
general editor.
      p. cm.
  Focus on the Family book
  ISBN-13: 978-1-58997-172-1
  ISBN-10: 1-58997-172-8
  1. Depression, Mental—Popular works. I. Title.
  RC537.H352 2006
  616.85'27—dc22
                                        2006011937

Printed in the United States of America
1 2 3 4 5 6 7 8 9 / 12 11 10 09 08 07 06

Contents

Foreword

This year nearly 10 million American adults will experience major depression. Perhaps you or someone you love is one of those individuals. If so, let me commend you for picking up this book. Admitting that depression is negatively affecting you or your family isn't easy—but by honestly facing the problem you've taken the first step toward wholeness and healing.

As a clinical psychologist I've worked with men, women, and teenagers whose lives have been severely affected by clinical depression. I've heard them describe overwhelming feelings of sadness, guilt, and worthlessness. I've known some people who felt so hopeless that they seriously considered ending their own lives.

I've also seen how the proper treatment of depression can restore hope and bring a renewed sense of joy and pleasure to life.

Help! Someone I Love Is Depressed will help you understand the causes, symptoms, and treatments for depression. It is written by my colleague Dr. Archibald Hart, a respected authority on depression and the former dean of the Fuller School of Psychology. Dr. Hart's book is clear, concise, and easy to read. Like a trusted friend, he'll guide you through the sometimes confusing world of mood disorders—leading you to a scientifically and spiritually accurate understanding of depression.

May God bless you as you begin your journey of hope!

Dr. Bill Maier
Vice President, Psychologist in Residence
Focus on the Family

Part One

Depression and Its Causes

Jana's story

After Jana's youngest child left for college, Jana's husband, Kyle, noticed gradual changes in her behavior. She began sleeping until noon, neglecting her appearance, and bingeing on junk foods she rarely touched before. Kyle would arrive home from work in the evening to find Jana still in her pajamas, the house a wreck, and dinner not started. She didn't seem to care about anything, didn't want to go anywhere, and didn't have any energy. What had happened to the woman who had taken such meticulous care of herself and her family—the woman who once had dozens of interests? Kyle suspected she was feeling overwhelmed by serious depression. But what could he do to help her?

☙ ☙ ☙

Depression is so epidemic in our society that it's been labeled the "common cold"

of emotions. At some time, one in every
five people will experience depression
seriously enough to hinder his or her normal way of life. It can increase feelings of
insecurity, low self-esteem, and helplessness. Left untreated, depression can crip-
ple a person emotionally and physically.

How can you detect its symptoms?
What steps can you take to overcome it?
How can you encourage a friend or loved
one who is depressed? What treatments
are available? This book was written to
answer those questions.

What Is Depression?

Depression is a feeling of gloom or sadness that is usually accompanied by a
slowing down of the body. It is experienced throughout a person's whole body,
not just in the mind as some people mis-
takenly believe.

Depression can be seen as a symptom, a disease, or a reaction. As a symptom, depression is part of the body's warning system, calling attention to something that's wrong. It tells us there has been a violation of some sort; something is missing or lost, or something is physically wrong.

But depression is also a disease in itself. It can be a serious consequence of stress in which the stress hormone cortisol is too high, or in its most severe form, the psychotic depressions, it is an illness category all its own. Known as a major depression, it has two forms: unipolar depression (one gets severely depressed) and bipolar depression (alternating manic [mentally hyperactive] and depressed moods).

Finally, depression can be a reaction to what is going on in life, or more specifically, to significant losses one experiences. This last form is known as reactive depression. It's the kind most people contend with in their daily lives. If we are emotionally healthy, we deal with those losses promptly, and the depression is short-lived. If we're not, the depression lingers and may even get worse or become chronic.

Categories of Depression

There are three major categories of depression: dysthymia, major depression, and bipolar disorder.

Dysthymia is a mild form of depression, but one that can persist for a long time. The symptoms include a loss of interest or pleasure in most if not all usual activities and pastimes. But it is typically not of sufficient severity and duration to be considered a major depression.

It has usually been around a long time (longer than two years) and while the sufferer may feel sad, blue or down in the dumps a lot of the time, there are periods when the mood feels normal. These normal periods may last a few days or a few weeks, then the sadness returns. It usually begins in early adulthood, but these days we are seeing more and more of it in children and teens. Dysthymia can easily develop into a lifelong pattern, and while it can be difficult to recognize, recent advances in diagnosis and antidepressant medications are making treatment more effective.

Major depression is often a debilitating disorder, and as the name implies, more serious. It can occur at almost any age. The sufferer typically is largely unemotional and withdrawn, is very sad, cries easily, feels unable to experience any pleasure, feels hopeless, helpless, and unworthy, has difficulty concentrating and focusing, and may complain that he or she doesn't "care anymore." There may be social withdrawal and apathy. There is often a serious disruption of sleep patterns (either insomnia or hypersomnia), changes in eating habits (eating either too much or not enough), and bouts of severe agitation. It can even manifest psychotic behaviors (severe mental impairments in one's thinking that are often very debilitating) such as delusions and hallucinations and serious death wishes. The depression can occur as a single episode, or in repeated episodes. This form of depression used to be called "endogenous depression," implying that it was from within the brain, or biological in its origin. We now know that it is caused by serious abnormalities in the regulation of neurotransmitters like serotonin, and can be enormously helped by appropriate antidepressant medications in conjunction with counseling.

Bipolar disorder is a form of depression in which there is an alternating mood that cycles from deep depression to a state of mania (inappropriate, and hyper-energetic activity). The cycle can be slow, changing every few months, or rapid, perhaps changing every few days. There is strong evidence that it may be genetic in origin and often starts before the age of 30. In some individuals there is considerable impairment in both social and occupational activities, and the sufferer can easily engage in inappropriate behaviors such as spending binges or sexual acting out followed by severe bouts of depression including contemplating suicide to the point where a plan for carrying it out is seriously considered or attempted. Where the mania is bizarre and excessive, the disorder is referred to as Type I, and where the mania is not severe or merely manifests as mildly excessive activities or restlessness, it is referred to as Type II. Both forms can be treated very effectively with a combination of medications.

Common Symptoms of Depression

Because depression can mimic many illnesses, it might go undiagnosed for a long time. The many illnesses it can mimic include general health problems, central nervous system disturbances, gastric problems, muscular problems, heart problems, respiratory problems, and even skin problems. Depression can present itself with anger, headaches, backaches, fatigue, irritability, hypersensitivity, and a whole range of disturbing sensations.

The gastrointestinal tract (stomach and colon) is a common site for depressive symptoms to manifest themselves. Food and alcohol are common tranquilizers used to cover depression. Sometimes a symptom may appear merely as a lump in the throat or difficulty swallowing.

Other symptoms that can mask depression include loss of libido; sexual dysfunction; excessive eating; possible weight loss; frequent throat clearing; intolerance to certain foods because of their texture; or swallowing excessive air, resulting in bloating. Common symptoms of depression include:

- Persistent sadness, anxiety, or an "empty" mood

- Feelings of hopelessness and pessimism
- Feelings of guilt, worthlessness, help- lessness (Depressed people may burst out crying for the slightest reason.)
- Loss of interest or pleasure in ordi- nary activities, including sex
- Sleep disturbances such as insom- nia, early morning waking, or oversleeping
- Eating disturbances (either loss or gain in appetite and weight)
- Decreased energy, fatigue, being slowed down
- Thoughts of death or suicide and even suicide attempts
- Restlessness and irritability
- Physical symptoms such as headaches, digestive disorders, and chronic pain that does not respond to treatment

- Difficulty in concentrating, remembering, and making decisions

Spiritual symptoms of depression are just as important as the physical and psychological ones. Spiritual symptoms can take two extremes. The most common is to pull away from God—to feel He is rejecting us. This reaction is triggered by the excessive psychological guilt one experiences in depression. Since we feel guilty, we assume God is punishing us by rejecting us. That irrational idea leads to spiritual withdrawal on our part.

The opposite reaction is to become overly involved in spiritual things. In a desperate attempt to regain normality or cope with the depression, a person may become fanatical about religious things to compensate for feelings of guilt. Unfortunately, this overinvolvement is not always healthy.

Stages of Depression

Depression is a continuum of feelings, ranging from minor blues to the most severe forms of mental illness. But that doesn't mean we go from one level to another. There are big jumps between the various levels of depression. The difference between a minor reactive depression and a severe psychotic depression, for example, is enormous. There's no connection between the two.

There are identifiable stages in a reactive depression, however. In the early stage we are usually busy analyzing whatever loss we've experienced. As we start this grieving process and the implications of the loss become more apparent, we find ourselves moving much deeper into depression. Finally, however, we "bottom out" and begin to put things into perspective as we come to terms with the loss.

This is the recovery phase.

We can't really speak of stages in the severe forms of depression. They come on suddenly and can deeply intensify in a matter of days. But they also stop rather suddenly, especially if they have been effectively treated.

Progression of Depression

Symptoms of depression can progress and intensify over time. Initially we may experience a low mood or a minor or temporary loss of interest in our environment, together with some feeling of discouragement. Usually our thinking isn't disturbed and remains rational. Physically, we may experience a knot in the pit of the stomach or other physical symptoms such as headaches, muscle and joint aches, and so on. Our eating and sleeping habits typically remain fairly normal. We may engage in some temporary spiritual withdrawal, but it's usually not significant.

As the symptoms of depression intensify, the feeling of hopelessness is much more dominant. There may be some crying, and it becomes difficult to focus and concentrate. As we become more preoccupied with ourselves, the depression seems to dominate our lives. There may be some appetite and sleep changes. Spiritually, there's a greater tendency to pull away from God.

As the depression progresses, everything already described occurs but is typically intensified. There's extreme sadness, low mood, dejection with frequent crying, extreme discouragement, and much guilt, self-blame, and self-pity. Physically, there's a disruption of appetite and sleep, with extremes of excess or privation. We become increasingly unable to cope with our environment and begin to neglect ourselves and our appearance. We find it extremely difficult to go about our regular duties. Spiritually, we withdraw from most activities, or we become intensely preoccupied with religious matters.

The Causes of Depression

Life is full of losses, and along the way we have to learn to deal with them. If we don't, we may become depression prone. In many respects, all losses are similar. It's just a matter of degree, and even though some of our more complex losses are more abstract, they can still be significant losses for the mind to cope with.

Some level of depression typically follows a significant loss. The depression may be slight, but it is often there.

We are all designed to experience emotion, including depression resulting from loss. If we can learn to cooperate with it, the grieving process can be a healthy response, even a healing emotion. The positive side of depression can be seen in two of its functions: It alerts us to a loss, and it helps us to detach from the lost object in a process of "letting go." Appropriate grieving is normal and necessary for healing.

Perhaps the best example I can give of this is in the experience of bereavement. A lot of evidence shows that the emotion of grief following bereavement must be allowed full expression for healing to occur. The more freedom we give ourselves to grieve, the more rapid is our recovery from the grief.

Depression can also be a positive factor in the physical realm. It is a symptom of many illnesses, including the flu. The depression aids in healing by detaching us from activity. If we didn't detach and slow down, the illness would further harm us. So our sadness and loss of interest in normal activities may aid the healing process.

Categories of Loss

It's helpful to put our losses in one of four categories: concrete, abstract, imagined, and threatened.

Concrete losses involve the loss of tangible objects. Examples include being in an automobile accident, dropping and breaking a camera, or losing a pet.

Abstract losses can be just as real as the first category of losses, but they're made up of intangibles such as the loss of love, ambition, self-respect, or control.

Imagined losses come from our active

imaginations. We can imagine both concrete and abstract losses. We imagine a friend has snubbed us or that someone dislikes us. These imaginings set us up for loss and depression just as if the actual loss has occurred.

Threatened losses have not actually taken place yet, so the grieving process cannot be completed. An example is the impending death of a loved one. You start feeling depressed, and the grieving process begins, but until the actual death takes place, you can't complete it. You will continue to feel depressed as long as the threat of loss exists.

The intensity of a depression is determined by the significance or meaning of the loss. The more meaningful the object lost, the greater the grief and the ensuing depression may be, and the greater the adjustment required to accept the loss.

This is why perhaps one of the deepest forms of depression follows the loss of a loved one in death.

Frequently, losses can accumulate. For example, if a child's parents divorce, it will provoke some anger and depression in the child. But suppose he then has to move to another state with one parent. Now he suffers additional losses, including his home, school, friends, the close proximity of the other parent, and any number of smaller losses. With one loss coming on top of another, his young mind will not be able to separate them and he will become very sensitive to loss and depression.

You can see how this accumulation of losses begins to create a significant cascade of emotions. One of the key principles we need to learn, therefore, is to minimize the accumulation of our losses and deal with them individually. The tendency to allow smaller losses to accumulate into bigger ones is often the result of having experienced many losses before. The more losses we've had earlier in life, particularly during childhood, the more likely we are to react to later losses with an exaggerated response.

To understand this type of depression, we must grasp the concept of loss and recognize how we're created to respond through the grieving process. We also need to understand the idea of "attachment." The greater our attachment to someone or something—and the more tightly we hold on—the greater will be the experience of depression.

Resolving depression, therefore, is a matter of "disconnecting" from the object to which we have become attached. The healing of depression ultimately comes when we allow the thing or person to which we're clinging to go free. That applies to everything from a person's reputation to disappointments to even one's need to be in control.

Physiological Causes of Depression

Hormonal and metabolic imbalances, fatigue caused by stress, and many illnesses, including cancer and influenza, can cause depression in both men and women. Many medications cause depression as well. In women, the menstrual cycle can be a very important cause. Some physiological causes are mysterious; we haven't yet discovered what they are, though we can see their effects.

In northern climates where sunlight is

minimal during certain seasons, residents may be plagued by a form of depression called Seasonal Affective Disorder (SAD). In these climates, doctors recommend that people affected by SAD spend a few minutes each day under specially designed "light bars," which effectively prevent depressive symptoms.

Some forms of depression are clearly hereditary. But even here, stress plays an aggravating role. Some hereditary tendencies might not ever express themselves if we keep our stress levels under control. Hereditary causes can be responsible for both major depressions and minor ones as well.

Some evidence suggests that in people who experience a psychological depression over a long period, the body becomes adapted to that lower level of functioning. The biochemical disturbance becomes relatively permanent, but it is brought about by a lifetime of depressive living.

Aging and Depression

Many midlife crises, especially in men, are triggered by depression, but the situation is much more complex than that. A midlife crisis may be both a cause and a consequence of depression for some people. It's best, perhaps, to view midlife crisis and depression as being bound together interdependently.

For some, growing old will be a traumatic experience. As both men and women approach the middle and final stages of life, they start to think about what they haven't achieved or what is still left to be done. That can be a source of significant depression.

Another common cause of depression in the elderly is the combination of medications taken for various physical ailments and diseases. It is important to inform the primary care provider of all medications that have been prescribed by all specialists, as well as any over-the-counter preparations the patient routinely takes. It also helps to fill all prescriptions at the same pharmacy so the pharmacist can monitor possible drug interactions.

Women and Depression

According to a report in the Stanford *Observer*, women suffer from serious depression at about twice the rate of men. There's a lot of argument about why that is. Many theories have been proposed, ranging from social conditions and income differences to biological reasons and hormones.

Risk Factors for Women

Psychological and biological factors often work in tandem to produce a given state of depression. What are these risk factors?

Living Alone. According to statistics, living alone doubles the risk of depression. To avoid being at increased risk for depression, single women and especially single mothers need to develop an adequate base of friendships and social contacts. Even married women can be socially isolated and extremely lonely. Such women, like single women, can be at increased risk for depression unless they build an adequate network of friends and participate in regular social activities outside the home.

Sexual Desirability. Our culture puts the primary responsibility on women to be attractive to men in order to date and marry. As a result, many women are at increased risk for depression if they don't see themselves as sexually desirable.

Lack of Identity. For many women, especially those who don't develop careers of their own, identities can become too wrapped up in the roles of mother and wife. If anything happens to disturb those roles or to take them away, depression can be a serious problem. Women who divorce later in life also experience this reaction of isolation and abandonment.

Premenstrual Syndrome and Depression

"Premenstrual syndrome" (the clinical term is premenstrual dysphonic disorder, or PMDD) may be a cause of biological depression in some women.

It is speculated that a major cause of PMS (PMDD) is the dramatic change in hormones around the time of menses. Hormonal changes may decrease sero-

tonin levels, which may cause depression.
The emotional effects of PMS that accompany the physical (such as headaches,
bloating, and pain) are fatigue, tension,
anxiety, and irritability. Many women
experience sadness and depression. They
feel listless and without energy. They lose
interest in normal activities, and they may
feel inadequate.

Menopause and Depression

Of all the causes for depression among
women, this is one of the most common.
It's associated with the change of life, and
not surprisingly, it affects *both* men and
women, though it is more serious in
women.

Menopause is the perfectly natural
cessation of the reproduction process.
Most menopausal problems are *entirely*
biological and have to do with the natural

decline of estrogen and the cessation of childbearing ability.

The primary symptoms of menopause are hot flashes, night sweats, irritability, depression, mood changes, insomnia, vaginal dryness, and short-term memory changes. Often, women who have menopause-related depression are unaware that they are depressed and don't fully appreciate the relationship between depression and menopause or perimenopause.

Postpartum Depression

It is relatively common for new mothers to experience the "baby blues," which often subside in the days following birth. For some women, feelings of depression persist and intensify, resulting in postpartum depression. If a new mother's depression has not lifted by her postpartum checkup, she should discuss it with her doctor during her office visit.

The intensity of postpartum symptoms can vary from mild, where a woman may feel a little down for a few days, to severe psychosis, where she is incapable of taking care of her child. The more severe the depression, the more clearly it is caused by biological factors. Some women have a period of depression following the birth of each child. Others have it only occasionally.

Almost every mother goes through a few "low" days after the birth of a child. This coincides roughly with the time it takes for the breasts to begin to produce milk. Many more women, however, experience a more severe depression when they leave the hospital.

Depression in Children and Adolescents

At any one time, as many as one in five children may be suffering from significant symptoms of depression. For many children, their depressions are temporary and don't require any special treatment. They are caused by normal losses every child has to come to terms with. Children lose pets; friends move away; relatives die; sometimes they are deeply disappointed when their expectations aren't met.

Childhood depressions can also be very serious, not only because of the intensity of the depressions, but also because children are almost totally incapable of responding to their environment and making the appropriate adjustments to loss.

Perhaps the most important point to make about childhood depression is that it's in those early stages of development that the patterns for later depressions are laid. The way a child comes to terms with frustration and learns how to handle loss sets the stage for how depressions are handled later in life, particularly in the neurotic and reactive depressions.

What Is Childhood Depression?

Some researchers will classify as a depression only a mood disorder that is totally incapacitating. On the other hand, I believe depression embraces the full range from a normal experience of sadness all the way through to a major depression. It's not always easy to draw a line between what's normal and what is clinically a problem. For a child, however, it probably doesn't make any difference. Depression is depression. And when a child is sad, what's important is that he or she learns how to deal with that sadness in a healthy manner.

Adults show their depression clearly as intense sadness, a tendency to cry a lot, loss of energy, and social withdrawal. But children don't always show their depression so straightforwardly. Here are some of the ways a child manifests depression:

- sadness
- withdrawal—the child will not converse or play with friends
- no interest in regular activities or games
- a profound loss of energy
- complaints about being tired all the time
- little capacity for pleasure
- many physical complaints, ranging from stomachache to headache to vague pains all over the body

- complaints about feeling unloved or rejected
- refusal to receive comfort or love, despite protests of not being loved
- many thoughts about death and dying
- an increase in aggressive behavior, bickering, and negativity
- many sleep disturbances, including insomnia
- a change in appetite, either over-eating or refusing to eat favorite foods

One factor in childhood depression that's different from adult depression is the increased sensitivity children have in relating to their peers. They are very concerned about how they're seen by friends, and any rejection they perceive causes or aggravates depression.

We need to be alert to the *hidden symptoms* of childhood depression. These include:

- extreme forms of anxiety
- nail biting
- hair pulling or twirling
- muscle tics
- irritability
- temper tantrums
- sulkiness or moodiness
- excessive negativity
- self-mutilation
- deliberate destructive behavior

There are many causes for childhood depression, but as with adult depression, the causes all reduce to one essential theme: the experience of loss. Biological depressions are not as common in children as they are in adolescents or adults. As a child approaches puberty, however, important hormonal changes may affect mood and produce temporary depressions. By and large, though, younger children are not being pushed and pulled by their hormones. They are being tugged at by life itself and the experience of loss.

By far the most serious cause of childhood depression is the divorce or separation of parents; it's particularly damaging to a child approaching puberty. Divorce represents many losses, including the separation of the family, loss of one parent, and perhaps a change in environment with a loss of friends. There are also many threatened losses as the child anxiously tries to anticipate the future.

Any experience of failure by a child can be the cause of depression because of the loss it represents. Not coping well at school, repeated failure, or an inability to perform at the same level as other children may seriously harm a child's self-image and self-esteem.

Parents who communicate extremely high standards to their children and the expectation that those standards be met may also foster a state of profound loss. Children who cannot live up to their parents' standards or who constantly feel rejected by parents because they're not "making it" may experience significant losses.

Adolescent Depression

We've known for a long time that adolescence is a period of extreme emotional discomfort. With the growing frequency of adolescent suicide, many experts now believe adolescent depression is far more common than adult depression. At least one out of every eight teens will experience significant depression sometime during the adolescent period.

Because adolescence is a period of emotional upheaval anyway, depression may be hard to recognize. Feelings of sadness, loneliness, anxiety, and hopelessness that are normally associated with depression may also be seen in the normal stresses of growing up. Some adolescents who are depressed act out their distress, becoming inappropriately angry or aggressive, running away, or becoming delinquent. Such behaviors can easily be dismissed as "typical adolescent storminess," and their significance in pointing to the presence of a serious depression is overlooked. Any of these signs, therefore, should be examined closely in case they indicate depression.

In determining whether an adolescent is depressed, we have to look at what changes have taken place. The following questions may help to clarify the state of the adolescent mind:

1. Has the once outgoing child become withdrawn and antisocial as an adolescent?

2. Was the adolescent formerly a good student but is now failing or skipping classes?

3. Was the child happy-go-lucky but is now moping around for weeks or months?

4. Is the teenager inappropriately irritable, whereas once he or she was calm and long-suffering?

If your answer is yes to any of these questions, it may indicate you need to get some help for your teenager. In addition, if your youngster feels unable to cope, demoralized, friendless, or is possibly suicidal, it's almost certain that he or she is depressed. An appetite disorder called anorexia nervosa, which involves a rejection of food and an avoidance of eating, is frequently a symptom of depression in girls (and occasionally in boys).

One of the complicating factors of depression in adolescence is that bipolar disorder often emerges. This is a serious form of depression. It is manifested by periods of impulsiveness, irritability, loss of control, and sometimes bizarre behavior when the teenager is unable to sleep and engages in a lot of meaningless manic behavior. Such a disorder needs immediate professional treatment.

Healing
for
Depression

Hope in the form of treatment options and professional help is available for those suffering from depression. Let's consider some of the ways you can help yourself or a friend or loved one who is depressed.

Professional Treatments for Depression

Even the most severe forms of depression can respond rapidly to treatment. Most treatments for depression are conducted in combination, which is often more effective than any one method by itself. Of course, treatment and results depend on the nature of the depression.

Psychotherapy

An important professional treatment is psychotherapy, or counseling, which provides guidance and insight in dealing with normal problems. Psychotherapy is a beneficial treatment in many depressions, and it may be used together with the other treatments (medication and rarely, ECT). The process of psychotherapy helps us to interpret what's going on in our lives and develop insight into our depression.

Therapy should not be restricted to what goes on in the formal, professional sense between a psychologist and a client. Developing and maintaining healthy relationships aids in psychotherapy success. A spouse and friends can be very helpful in providing understanding, and later we'll examine how they can do that well.

But there are limitations to the help a nonprofessional person can provide. Untrained people should not assume the role of a psychotherapist. They're not equipped to understand how certain psychological functions interact or how defenses of various sorts operate. For these reasons, unless the problem is relatively minor, it's often better to go to a professional.

Clergy who are well trained as counselors can provide effective help for minor depressions and referrals to other professionals. Many clergy are not trained to counsel, however. They should know when they've reached the limits of their capabilities in specific situations and should then refer people to more specialized help.

If you have a good relationship with a medical doctor, that may be a good place to begin.

Medication

Another beneficial, and often necessary, treatment is the use of antidepressant medication. Medication can be prescribed by a primary care provider such as a family doctor, internist, or gynecologist, or by a psychiatrist, sometimes in consultation with a clinical psychologist.

If medication is prescribed, it is imperative that the patient have regularly scheduled follow-up appointments to reevaluate the depression and treatment. Occasionally different medications or combinations of medications may need to be used. Most antidepressants require a steady buildup before significant improvement is apparent, averaging from two to six weeks. For some people it may take less or more time before the full effect of the medication is felt. By the same token, people should never just stop taking antidepressants suddenly. They should be phased out slowly over a period of three weeks or so.

Electroconvulsive Therapy

A third category of treatment is the use of electroconvulsive therapy (ECT). It is, unfortunately, grossly misunderstood. It involves giving the brain an electrical impulse that causes a mild seizure while the patient is anesthetized. ECT is remarkably effective in treating certain severe depressions. Unfortunately, many people avoid this type of treatment because of misconceptions about its use.

Fear and misunderstanding are the basis of the controversy. In the past, ECT was used on a wide variety of people in mental institutions, sometimes without proper permission and inappropriately. That has left some people with lingering suspicions based on horror stories they've heard. The media have not been particularly helpful in this regard, tending to perpetuate misconceptions about ECT.

This form of treatment is reserved for use by psychiatrists specializing in the forms of mental illness that can be treated by ECT.

When Should Someone Seek Professional Help?

Sometimes people find that their depression is lasting longer than they feel comfortable about, or they find themselves deeply depressed. They may begin to think of ways of escaping, avoiding family responsibilities, or they may even consider suicide. The time has come to seek professional help.

Sometimes, too, depressions coexist with severe physiological reactions, and the grieving process is contaminated by biological disturbances. The person then needs professional help to sort out what's psychological and what's biological and to facilitate recovery.

With the onset of a medium-intensity depression, the help that just talking to a friend can give has reached its limit. As the intensity increases, the risk that depressed people will take their own lives increases. There's also a greater likelihood of biological depression. When people begin to cry often and feel their situation is hopeless, they definitely need professional help.

If you believe a friend should see a professional therapist, and if the person is not your spouse, you first need to consult with those closest to him or her—a spouse or significant relative. You all need to be in agreement on what action should be recommended. It is far better if the direction comes from those closest to the depressed person. If you're the closest person or there is no one but you, you need to discuss your concerns in a straightforward manner. Be sure to put it in the context of your love and care for your friend or relative; don't present it in a critical or judgmental way.

If you get an angry response, you need to work through that anger together. Receive it—don't draw away or become offended.

Helping a Depressed Friend or Loved One

The material in this section is specifically presented to guide you as you seek to give the most effective understanding and support possible to a depressed friend, spouse, or child. It is not designed to take the place of professional help, but to make you a wiser and more empathetic helper. If you're in close contact with a depressed person, you'll be an important part of the healing process whether you want to be or not.

Remember that depression saps energy and self-esteem and interferes with a person's ability or wish to get help. If someone you know shows symptoms of depression but hasn't talked to you about it, show your love and concern by drawing that person aside and gently encouraging him or her to talk to you. Often there's a sense of relief when someone approaches and says, "I can see you're hurting. Why don't you discuss it with me so we can be in this together?" That's all a person needs sometimes to take the first step toward getting help.

When people are depressed, they're

very sensitive to relationships. Sometimes the very closeness of a relationship makes the person uncomfortable with discussing problems. If this is the case with your friend or loved one, don't take it personally.

The nature of the help you can offer may change through the different phases of the depression, but the help should always be there, assuming you have the proper rapport with the person. If he or she is a stranger or a distant friend, you should realize you haven't yet earned the right to become involved.

Unless you've been taught to recognize symptoms of depression, it's difficult to catch depression early, because it usually comes on rapidly. By the time you see it, it's fully developed. If some loss has occurred, the person *needs* to be depressed. The depression will come despite your best intentions. What you do during the depression is much more important than trying to prevent or abort it.

In your first contact with a depressed person, the most important thing is to communicate understanding and acceptance. The person's encounter with most people will lead him to believe his depression is not acceptable, that he should feel guilty about being depressed, and that he should not really be depressed at all. Again, it is vital to communicate love and acceptance and avoid being judgmental.

Obviously, there is a place for confrontation in real relationships, but avoid using confrontation as a general style. Confrontation is often damaging, because it's usually done with an element of anger and frustration. We want to rush in because something looks so obvious from our perspective, but we don't always understand the full context. It is far better to hold back and first try to be understanding. That earns you the right to confront later. A qualified exception would be during the recovery phase of the depression. Then a low-key confrontation—gentle prodding and pushing—may be helpful. Whatever else you do, do not try to talk the person out of being depressed.

It's important that the depressed person identify the source of his or her depression. In providing a listening ear, you can help the person explore the possible causes and understand better the events that may have initiated it. Of course, if you see something obvious that's being overlooked, you should present this to the person. In doing so, present it in the form of a question rather than a dogmatic statement. Using a question allows the person to reflect. If the notion is rejected, you can come back a little later and ask the question again.

Active listening is the key technique here, not cross-questioning or probing. That means you are constantly checking out what you're hearing by reflecting it back to your friend or loved one in a process of clarification: "Now is this what you mean?"

Encourage the person to seek appropriate psychological and medical care, and support the course of recommended treatment.

You need not be a professional counselor to do these things, but you may disqualify yourself as a helpful counselor if you become too personally and emotionally involved with the depression. If the person's loss triggers in you too many insecure feelings, you should back off.

Depressed people need help from someone who can be impartial.

Spiritual Misunderstandings about Depression

A common mistake on the part of some Christians is to insist that all depressions are spiritual. The tendency to spiritualize all depressions is dangerous. Spiritualizing depression is too simplistic and is certainly not scriptural. Many people sin but never get depressed, and many Christians who have not necessarily sinned get depressed. The best we can say is that sometimes there is a connection between sin and depression, but not always.

Another common mistake is to think of depression as being caused or perpetuated by lack of faith in God. This implies that if a person were deeply spiritual, he or she would not get depressed or would get over the depression quickly. If he or she doesn't, he or she is a spiritual failure.

Another common idea is that healing from depression is exclusively a spiritual exercise. Some preach and teach that all depression is healed by simply confessing it, repenting of it, and turning back to God. This idea fails to recognize that many of our depressions have roots in biochemical or genetic causes, or that a legitimate spiritual discipline needs to be exercised through our depressions. I am a strong believer that God can help us in the healing process and that when it's an entirely spiritual matter, He provides the healing. But in many instances, people need help in addition to whatever prayer or confession they need to make.

Recognizing Suicidal Tendencies

It's not always easy to recognize suicidal tendencies because if people are intending suicide, they often become secretive, withdraw, and won't talk to anyone. On the other hand, there's frequently a "cry for help" in some action. Contrary to myth, it's not true that if a person talks about suicide, he or she won't do it. Many make statements such as, "I wish I were dead." Some even tell a friend about a plan to kill themselves before they do it. If a friend or loved one talks like that, take it seriously. If she wants to talk about suicide, by all means encourage her to do so.

Signs that someone is contemplating suicide include:

- a change in behavior such as losing interest in family, friends, hobbies, and so on

- becoming more careless about personal appearance, giving things and money away, buying a gun or stockpiling pills
- becoming more lethargic, losing appetite, expressing more anger.
- expressing intense anger over a major loss

Loved ones and caregivers should pay particular attention to the following:

- Prior suicide attempts
- A family history of suicide
- A history of substance abuse
- Psychosis
- General or severe medical illness
- Advanced age
- A profound sense of helplessness

If you feel a person is depressed but not talking about suicide, ask him to express his thoughts about death. Watch for signs of secretiveness, hostility, or aggression. The suicidal person often has a lot of hostility that can't be expressed. Anything you can do to help the person talk about this anger will be helpful.

If you determine that your loved one may be suicidal, don't hesitate to take appropriate action. It will be helpful to remove any dangers such as medications, guns, ammunition, and so on from the home.

If you believe suicide is imminent, immediately consult your primary care provider or take your loved one to the emergency room. If these attempts fail, call 911. Do not leave the depressed person alone until you can get help.

Helping Your Depressed Spouse

Couples need to accept that there's a limit to what counseling can be done between spouses. I encourage couples not to try counseling each other. You can't remain impartial and detached. Just accepting that limitation can go a long way toward avoiding the guilt of not being able to help. It also frees your spouse to seek counsel with someone else.

People with very severe depressions won't want to seek help. You will need to exert control in such a situation. Of course you shouldn't resort to force until you've exhausted all other means of reasoning and persuasion. Point out that the depression is not only destructive to him or her, but to everyone around as well. If you consult a professional psychologist or psychiatrist, your legal rights to enforce treatment will be explained.

Should you tell your parents and in-laws that your spouse is receiving treatment for depression? As a general rule, I believe in total honesty. I don't see any value in concealing the fact that your spouse is seeking help, although you may have to make an exception where parents are not understanding. Usually, though, the more people who know about it, the more love and encouragement your spouse can receive from them. However, if your spouse does not want to disclose this information, you should respect his or her confidentiality.

Help for an Elderly Loved One

Depression does not have to be a part of aging, but many elderly people do get depressed. Not only do their bodies change, limiting their ability to function as they did in the past, but many elderly also begin to feel a shortness of time. A sense of things coming to an end increases one's awareness of the limits of life. Side effects from certain medications can also contribute to depression.

While senility and depression are different phenomena, it can be difficult to separate the two. Senile disorders contribute to depression, though how much is physiological and how much is psychological isn't always clear. When a person suffers from a disorder like Alzheimer's disease, losses of friends and activities can trigger depression, as can the physical changes that occur in the brain.

It's important to start with a comprehensive medical evaluation, and then help the elderly person pursue the physician's recommendations, whether they include antidepressant medicines, vitamins and exercise, psychotherapy, or other treatments mentioned elsewhere in this book. Then provide understanding, affection, and encouragement. Whatever you do in response to an elderly friend or loved one's depression, don't ignore it.

Help for Women in Depression

Homemakers may be especially prone to depression due to isolation and the repetitive nature of homemaking. While I highly value the role of motherhood and of building and maintaining a happy home, homemakers should be encouraged to develop a stronger sense of identity outside the home. Without an identity broader than taking care of home and family, some women can be at risk for depression. This is not to say that many homemakers do not find a satisfying identity in being wives and mothers, but that it is a demanding job.

Women who work outside the home may lack stimulation too, due to trying to keep up with both workplace and family and feeling that they have no time for personal development. Therefore, the following suggestions can be helpful to any woman:

- If it's feasible, go back to school and enjoy the personal growth and mind enhancement education can provide.
- Become an avid reader. Books are a wonderful resource for expanding your mind and developing your identity.
- If time allows, engage in volunteer work and give yourself in service to people outside your home and/or workplace.
- Maintain a strong commitment to spiritual development, which addresses issues of identity and provides a much broader perspective

on our lives and on the function
and roles we play in the lives of
family members.

- If you are married, keep communication open with your husband
about your needs for identity and to
feel you are a growing person.

- Develop friendships with other
women. The understanding and
empathy of someone who's "been
there" can help you put your situation in perspective.

Help for PMS (PMDD)

Not every woman suffers acutely from
PMS, but many do. One doctor has heard
patients describe PMS this way: "Something comes in and takes control of me
and I can't do anything about it." For
these women, PMS can be a significant
problem. Here are some strategies that

may help relieve some of the symptoms of PMS:

Dietary changes. The right kinds of changes in diet can help significantly in lowering your mood swings. Some have found it helpful to eat more but smaller meals each day during the premenstrual period, keeping the calorie intake the same but not loading the gastrointestinal system with large meals. This helps to stabilize blood-sugar levels.

The unpleasant physical symptoms of PMS can be relieved by other minor changes. For example, bloating, painful breasts, weight gain, and headaches often result from water retention. By minimizing the bloating with, for example, increased water consumption in conjunction with a diet low in carbohydrates and salt, you can reduce the physical discomfort and may improve your mood.

Exercise. Regular exercise in any of its forms clearly benefits women with PMS because it helps to tone up the body and aids in relaxation. It also helps to burn off surplus adrenaline, thus lowering stress levels. Exercise also releases endorphins (natural opiates) into the bloodstream that decrease pain and cause feelings of pleasure and enjoyment.

Stress control. Stress significantly aggravates the problem of PMS. During times of high stress, adrenaline levels increase, muscle tension goes up, and blood volume is shifted within the body to those regions that require it for the emergency response (the brain, muscles, and lungs). Those changes, taken together, will reduce the body's ability to cope with the primary hormonal defi- ciency that underlies PMS. Good stress management is thus essential, as is learning effective relaxation exercises that will help to lower the body's adrenaline level and reduce its emergency mode.

Relaxation can be achieved by spending around 30 minutes a day in a quiet place, totally relaxing your body and mind. Starting with your feet, tense the foot muscles for five seconds, then relax them. Proceed up the body and through the various muscle systems, first tensing them for five seconds and then relaxing them, until you have covered the whole body. Having done that, remain immobile for the balance of the relaxation time. At the end of the time, take a few deep breaths and go about your business.

Another form of treatment that is helpful for some women is the use of anti-depressant medication. This can be prescribed by your primary care provider and must be monitored at regular intervals.

Help for Menopausal Depression

If a woman is struggling with menopausal depression, she should consult a gynecologist, since this physician is especially trained to deal with the problems of menopause. Another good place to start is with her primary care physician since he or she will be familiar with her health history and may already have a rapport with her.

In treating menopausal depression, keep two important aspects constantly in mind: the physiological aspect of diminished hormones, often involving dramatic symptoms such as "hot flashes" and disrupted sleep, as well as the psychological aspect. The combination of these can result in significant depression for some women.

It is very possible, therefore, that the treating physician may suggest the patient seek counseling or psychotherapy as a part of the treatment package. If the physician recommends that, or if a woman feels a lot of her depression is being caused by menopausal symptoms she isn't coping with satisfactorily, she should seek out a counselor or psychologist.

The use of medications such as hormonal therapy or antidepressants can be helpful in the treatment of menopausal symptoms and depression.

Help for Postpartum Depression

Among the most common feelings experienced in postpartum depression are insecurity, fear of inability to cope with the baby, disappointment about the child's sex or appearance, confusion, general fears, and anxiety.

New mothers with postpartum depression need to resist believing there is something wrong with them. Certainly, there may be something wrong with their hormones, but that doesn't reflect on them as people.

A brief period of counseling may be extremely helpful. If a woman can receive emotional support and reassurance from her family, friends, husband, mother, or counselor, the chances are that the depression will quickly pass and her recovery will be complete.

Husbands play a critical role in helping their wives deal with postpartum depression. A husband who knows what to look for can be the first line of defense in recognizing the symptoms of this disorder and getting his wife the professional help she needs.

Whatever you do, don't overglorify motherhood by expecting every new mom to measure up to some stereotype of the ideal mother. Being a mother is hard work, and not every baby is the perfect child. Just accepting the reality of what it takes to be a mother will help her cope a lot better.

Helping Your Depressed Child or Teenager

There are things we can do to help our children learn to deal well with loss and emerge from depression stronger, healthier persons. Begin by teaching them sound values. Early in life they need to learn not to give too much worth to material things. That helps to minimize the growth of an exaggerated sense of loss over them.

It's important, too, that we build our children's self-respect and self-esteem. We need to provide experimentation with a wide variety of interests and help them discover their strengths. Encourage your kids to find something they can do well so that they can feel a sense of mastery and accomplishment about it.

Furthermore, teach your kids how to delay gratification. By this I mean they should be taught that all their needs cannot be met immediately. There's a tendency in our culture to expect to have our needs satisfied instantly. That sets us up for a lot of frustration and depression, because life just doesn't work that way.

If you sense your child is depressed, the most important thing is to open up communication. You must allow your children the freedom to talk about their feelings of sadness and grieve their losses. This can bring to light some significant factors in their environment that may be contributing to their depression.

The first step in getting help is, of course, to get your child to acknowledge the depression. That isn't always easy. You may want to talk it over with your spouse, a close friend, or a member of the clergy before you confront your child. Alternatively, take your child to your family physician, and have him or her explain the problem.

If you determine that your child needs professional help, how you proceed after that depends on the age of the child. Young children are usually quite compliant. Taking them to a professional for help, provided you prepare them adequately and don't intensify their anxiety, should not be a problem. Many psychologists and psychiatrists specialize in childhood disorders. They know how to talk to children and how to make the experience pleasant. If you don't feel comfortable with the first professional you consult, move to someone else.

The older the child, the more difficult it may be to get appropriate help. A depressed 10- or 12-year-old may be quite resistant to going to see a professional, and you certainly cannot expect a child of that age to go alone. Make sure you or your spouse accompanies the child to provide a comforting source of reference. Children may be less resistant to seeing the family practitioner or pediatrician than a therapist.

The risk of suicide increases the older the child becomes and is particularly hazardous in the adolescent years. It's imperative that a depressed adolescent be seen by a mental health professional as soon as possible. A teenager may resist treatment, so it may be necessary for you, as a parent, to "get tough" or use some form of coercion.

In this regard, teenagers are extremely astute, even uncanny, in their ability to know if parents feel guilty or ambivalent about getting help for them. They can sense your indecisiveness, so you should, as parents, make up your minds about what you want to do. Then communicate an absolute sense of togetherness when it comes to telling your teenager you want him or her to get help.

Sometimes it's wise for parents to seek help for themselves before they approach their depressed child. However, if the child is destructive of self or others, it is essential that you don't delay. If you suspect that your teen might be suicidal, it is far better to get help, even if it turns out to be unnecessary, than afterward to regret not having taken any action. You'll have a lot less guilt to deal with if you act prematurely than if you do not act at all.

Remember that a depressive disorder is not a passing bad mood but an illness that can and should be treated. Adolescent depression is a serious disorder with serious consequences. Don't hesitate to get appropriate help.

Conclusion

Having read through this material on depression, you have seen two major themes: First, depression is often an appropriate emotion following a loss or as a result of a physiological imbalance. Second, communicating understanding and acceptance is the key to the effective support of a depressed person. The second theme clearly rests on the first, for if you won't accept depression as an inevitable experience of life, you can't give the empathetic support that will help to resolve the depression.

I would encourage you, as a concerned helper, to persist in developing an understanding of depression. But more importantly, I urge you to work at communicating understanding and acceptance of a depressed friend or relative in the context of love. That is your moral responsibility. But it's also a responsibility that God wants to help you meet. Don't forget to ask for His guidance and strength.

Resources

BOOKS

Brestin, Dee. *The Friendships of Women: Overcoming the Pain and Releasing the Power.* Colorado Springs, Colo.: Cook Communications.

Carter, Les, Ph.D., and Frank Minirth, M.D. *The Freedom from Depression Workbook.* Nashville, Tenn.: Thomas Nelson, 1995.

Cloud, Dr. Henry. *Changes that Heal: How to Understand the Past to Ensure a Healthier Future.* Grand Rapids, Mich.: Zondervan, 1997.

Hagerman, Nancy L. *In the Pit: A Testimony of God's Faithfulness to a Bipolar Christian.* Belleville, Ontario: Essence Publishing, 2001.

Hart, Dr. Archibald, and Dr. Catherine Hart Weber. *Stressed or Depressed: A Practical Guide for Parents of Hurting Teens.* Brentwood, Tenn.: Integrity Publishers, 2005.

Hart, Archibald D. *Unmasking Male Depression: Recognizing the Root Cause to Many Behaviors, Such as Anger, Resentment, Abusiveness, Silence, Addictions, and Sexual Compulsions.* Nashville, Tenn.: W Publishing Group, 2001.

Hart, Dr. Archibald and Dr. Catherine Hart Weber. *Unveiling Depression in Women: A Practical Guide to Understanding and Overcoming Depression.* Grand Rapids, Mich.: Revell, 2002.

Lush, Jean and Pam Vredevelt. *Women and Stress: A Practical Approach to Managing Tension.* Grand Rapids, Mich.: Revell, 1997.

Murphy, Dr. Tim and Loriann Hoff Oberlin. *The Angry Child: Regaining Control when Your Child Is Out of Control.* Three Rivers, Mich.: Three Rivers Press, 2002.

Sutton, Mark and Bruce Hennigan, M.D. *Conquering Depression: A 30-Day Plan to Finding Happiness.* Nashville, Tenn.: Broadman & Holman Publishers, 2001.

FOCUS ON THE FAMILY BROADCASTS (AVAILABLE ON CD)

Barnhill, Julie Ann. "Help for Angry Moms," CD162.

Blitchington, Dr. Peter. "A Christian Woman's Search for Self-Esteem," CS293.

Brestin, Dee. "Women and Friendships," CS439.

Dobson, Dr. James and panel. "Men in Mid-Life Reevaluation," CD129.

Hart, Archibald D. "Understanding Depression," CS636.

Lush, Jean. "The Stages of a Woman's Life," CD118.

Lush, Jean. "Women and Stress," CS748.

Maier, Dr. Bill and panel. "Teens in Crisis: Why Parents Matter," B00020D.

Wright, Dr. H. Norman. "A Counselor Looks at Depression," CS636.

FOCUS ON THE FAMILY BOOKLETS

Hart, Archibald D. *Depression: Help for Those Who Hurt*, LF192.

Horton, Marilee, et al. *Restoring Balance to your Life* (Women), LF205.

Seamands, David. *Letting Go of Painful Memories*, LF159.

INFORMATION SHEETS

"Coping with Mental Illness," FX256.

"Mental Illness," FX406.

"Resource List: Grief and Loss," RL045.

To order resources, speak to a counselor, or locate a Christian counselor in your area, call 1-800-AFAMILY (1-800-232-6459) between 9 A.M. and 4:30 P.M. Mountain Time, Monday through Friday. Our counseling department phone number is 719-531-5181. Please be aware that a counselor may not be immediately available and may have to return your call.

Dr. Bill Maier is Focus on the Family's vice president and psychologist in residence. Dr. Maier received his master's and doctoral degrees from the Rosemead School of Psychology at Biola University in La Mirada, California. A child and family psychologist, Dr. Maier hosts the national "Weekend Magazine" radio program and the "Family Minute with Dr. Bill Maier." He also acts as a media spokesperson for Focus on the Family on a variety of family-related issues. He and his wife, Lisa, have been married for more than seven years and have two children.

ɔ ɔ ɔ

Dr. Archibald Hart, Senior Professor of Psychology and Dean Emeritus of the School of Psychology at Fuller Theological Seminary, is also a well-known author of 25 books, including *Stressed or Depressed* (coauthored by Dr. Catherine Weber, his daughter). He and his wife, Kathleen, are sought after by church groups around the world to speak and conduct workshops on topics such as marriage, stress management, handling emotions, and the hazards of ministry.

FOCUS ^{ON}_{THE} FAMILY®

Welcome to the family!

Whether you purchased this book, borrowed it, or received it as a gift, we're glad you're reading it. It's just one of the many helpful, encouraging, and biblically based resources produced by Focus on the Family for people in all stages of life.

Focus began in 1977 with the vision of one man, Dr. James Dobson, a licensed psychologist and author of numerous best-selling books on marriage, parenting, and family. Alarmed by the societal, political, and economic pressures that were threatening the existence of the American family, Dr. Dobson founded Focus on the Family with one employee and a once-a-week radio broadcast aired on 36 stations.

Now an international organization reaching millions of people daily, Focus on the Family is dedicated to preserving values and strengthening and encouraging families through the life-changing message of Jesus Christ.

Focus on the Family Magazines

These faith-building, character-developing publications address the interests, issues, concerns, and challenges faced by every member of your family from preschool through the senior years.

| Focus on the Family **Citizen®** U.S. news issues | Focus on the Family **Clubhouse Jr.™** Ages 4 to 8 | Focus on the Family **Clubhouse™** Ages 8 to 12 | **Breakaway®** Teen guys | **Brio®** Teen girls 12 to 16 | **Brio & Beyond®** Teen girls 16 to 19 | **Plugged In®** Reviews movies, music, TV |

FOR MORE INFORMATION

Online:
Log on to www.family.org
In Canada, log on to
www.focusonthefamily.ca

Phone:
Call toll free: (800) A-FAMILY
In Canada, call toll free:
(800) 661-9800

More Great Resources
from Focus on the Family®